Clarinet Solos

Order No. AM40155
ISBN 978-0-8256-2028-7

Visit Hal Leonard Online at
www.halleonard.com

World headquarters, contact:
Hal Leonard
7777 West Bluemound Road
Milwaukee, WI 53213
Email: info@halleonard.com

In Europe, contact:
Hal Leonard Europe Limited
1 Red Place
London, W1K 6PL
Email: info@halleonardeurope.com

In Australia, contact:
Hal Leonard Australia Pty. Ltd.
4 Lentara Court
Cheltenham, Victoria, 3192 Australia
Email: info@halleonard.com.au

Everybody's Favorite Series No. 28

Clarinet Solos

CONTENTS

Clarinet Solos

CONTENTS BY COMPOSERS

Rêverie

CLAUDE DEBUSSY

Berceuse
(From "JOCELYN")

B. GODARD

None But the Lonely Heart

TSCHAIKOWSKY

Beautiful Dreamer

STEPHEN FOSTER

American Songs

I. Dixie

II. Swanee River

III. Oh Susanna

Allegretto

Valse Triste

SIBELIUS

Barcarolle
(From "TALES OF HOFFMAN")

OFFENBACH

I'll Take You Home Again, Kathleen

T. P. WESTENDORF

Jingle Bells

Cradle Song

BRAHMS

Drink to Me Only with Thine Eyes

ARNE

Chanson Triste

TSCHAIKOWSKY, Op. 40, No. 2

Melody in F

ANTON RUBINSTEIN

Minuet in G

L. VAN BEETHOVEN

Minuet D.C.

Ah! So Pure
(MARTHA)

VON FLOTOW

Ciribiribin

A. PESTALOZZA

Serenade

FRANZ SCHUBERT

Spring Song
(SONGS WITHOUT WORDS. No. 30)

F. MENDELSSOHN

Blue Danube Waltz

INTRO.
Andantino

J. STRAUSS

D.S. senza repetizione al Fine
(From sign without repetition to Fine)

Andante
(From the "5TH SYMPHONY")

TSCHAIKOWSKY

Cantique de Noel

A. ADAMS

Silent Night

F. GRÜBER

Cielito Lindo
(BEAUTIFUL HEAVEN)

C. FERNANDEZ

America

S. F. SMITH

Star Spangled Banner

FRANCIS SCOTT KEY

Adeste Fideles
(O COME, ALL YE FAITHFUL)

READING

Maestoso

Lead Kindly Light

J. B. DYKES

Onward Christian Soldiers

SIR ARTHUR SULLIVAN

Dancing Doll
(POUPEE VALSANTE)

ED. POLDINI

Habanera
(From "CARMEN")

G. BIZET

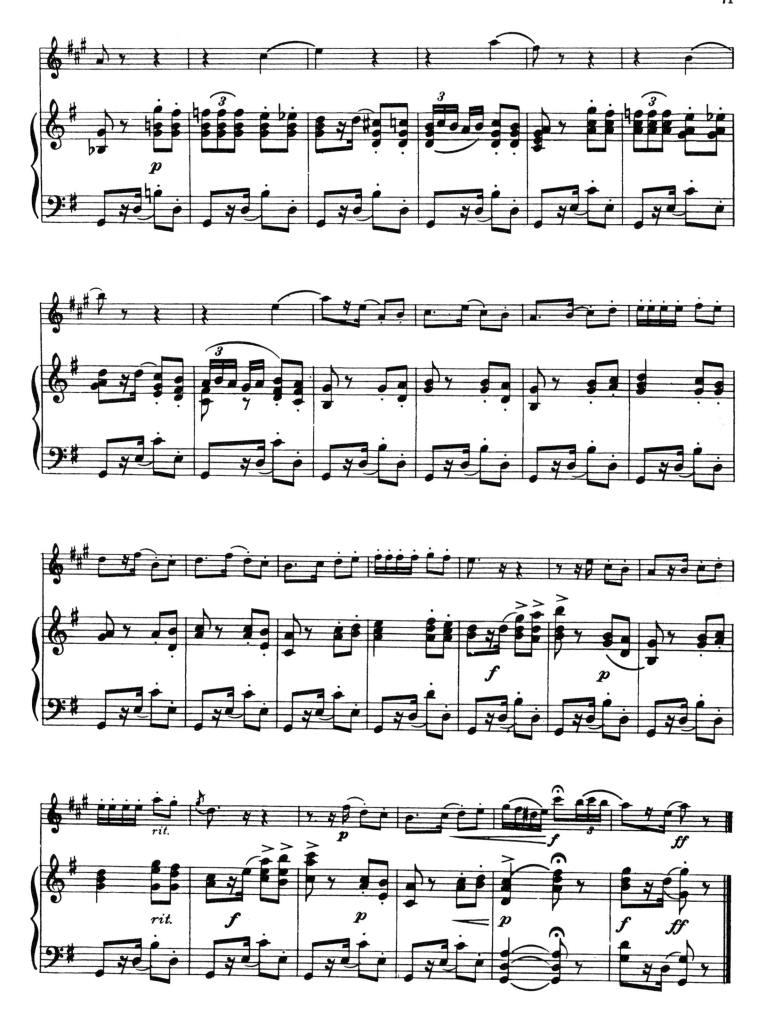

Song Without Words

TSCHAIKOWSKY

Clarinet Polka
(DZIA DUNIO)

Elegie

J. MASSENET

Dark Eyes
(OTCHE CHORNIA)

Russian Song

Viennese Refrain

Popular

Londonderry Air

Irish Folk Song

Gavotte

F. J. GOSSEC

Ave Maria

F. SCHUBERT

Molto adagio e religoso

Orientale
(THE KALEIDOSCOPE)

CESAR CUI, Op. 50

Romance

A. RUBINSTEIN, Op. 44

Nocturne

F. CHOPIN, Op. 9, No. 2

Hungarian Dance
No. 5

J. BRAHMS

Spanish Dance

M. MOSZKOWSKI

Humoreske

Poco lento e grazioso

ANTON DVOŘÁK, Op. 101, No. 7

Flight of the Bumble-Bee

N. RIMSKY - KORSAKOFF

Angel's Serenade

G. BRAGA

Souvenir

FRANZ DRDLA

Serenade

FRANZ DRDLA

Two Guitars

Russian Gypsy Folk Song

Hymn to the Sun

N. RIMSKY - KORSAKOFF

Irish Washerwoman
(JIG)

Arkansas Traveller
(COUNTRY DANCE)

Pop Goes the Weasel
(VIRGINIA REEL)

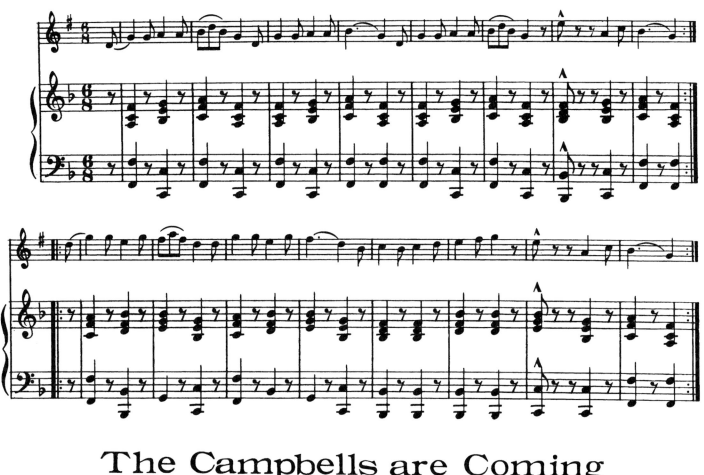

The Campbells are Coming
(SCOTCH DANCE)

Garry Owen
(IRISH JIG)

Paddy Whack
(IRISH JIG)

Money Musk
(REEL)

Sailor's Hornpipe
(COLLEGE)

Fisher's Hornpipe

Kerry Dance
(IRISH JIG)